Shattered Dreams

The Heartache and Enduring Hope of a Forsaken Wife

Matilda Kauffman

ISBN-13: 978-1-932676-24-2
ISBN-10: 1-932676-24-4

Printed in the United States of America

Layout & Cover Design: Lanette Steiner

Digital text entry: Elizabeth Burkholder

All Scriptures taken from the King James Version
unless otherwise indicated.

For information regarding bulk purchases, please contact:
Vision Publishers orders at 1-877-488-0901
Vision Publishers at P.O. Box 190, Harrisonburg, 22803

For information or comment, write to:
Vision Publishers
P.O. Box 190
Harrisonburg, VA 22803
Phone: 877/488-0901
Fax: 540/437-1969
E-mail: orders@vision-publishers.com
www.vision-publishers.com
(see order form in back)

A portion of each sale goes toward the support of
Matilda Kauffman.

Harrisonburg, VA

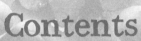

Contents

Shattered Dreams

Preface

The tragedy of a husband deserting his family is the ultimate nightmare for a devoted wife. If you have been handed such a faith-defying struggle, this book is for you. Or perhaps your husband is still with you, but your marriage is on the rocks. What can you do? Where can you turn? How can you experience peace, true happiness, and quietness of mind in the midst of an emotional storm that threatens to tear you down mentally, physically, and spiritually? What does Jesus ask of you, and is following His way even possible?

Admittedly, these situations generate much confusion as well as deep wounds and hurts. God is not the author of confusion but of peace, joy, and happiness. How does He accomplish this?

I want to share a few things I have learned through much trial and error while traveling through the deep, dark valley of sorrow and rejection, cast out by the man I vowed to love, and still do love.

In the early years of my marriage, I had the most thoughtful and loving husband. That's why my heart was completely crushed and broken when our marriage turned out as it did. We had been so close. I groped for answers, but found none.

Divorce was absolutely not an option in my mind. I believed it to be a grave sin in God's sight. Marriage is for life. God says, "So guard yourself in your spirit, and do not break faith with the wife of your youth. 'I hate divorce,' says the Lord God of Israel . . ." (Malachi 2:15, 16, NIV).

Where had I failed so desperately? My mind whirled, like a dog chasing its tail. My thoughts got me nowhere.

Does the Bible have answers? It does indeed. Although the answers are not always spelled out in black and white, the Bible offers basic principles to follow. One may be too blinded or hurt to see them, or maybe unwilling to believe they could work for a particular situation, but I believe the answers do exist.

With God's unfailing love and grace, I once again found peace and joy in my heart despite the underlying pain. True joy does not come from our circumstances but from following principles of almighty God and cleansing our souls before Him.

My deepest desire is to bring a ray of hope and inspiration to a sad or questioning heart as I share with you what God has taught me. I want to be a friend to anyone I meet on this lonely path.

> Blessed be God, even the Father of our Lord Jesus Christ, the Father of mercies, and the God of all comfort; who comforteth us in all our tribulations, that we may be able to comfort them which are in any trouble, by the comfort wherewith we ourselves are comforted of God (2 Corinthians 1:3, 4).

God truly has been wonderful in His dealings with me. May He comfort you as He comforted me.

—Matilda Kauffman

Introduction

A famous lecturer pulled a special bookmark from her Bible and held it up as she described her degrading experiences in a Nazi concentration camp. The audience saw only an ugly, tangled mass of different-colored yarn. Then, while telling the many benefits of her suffering, the speaker turned the marker. Now the audience saw the gorgeous needlework on the other side that said "God Is Love."

This story also begins with a confusing tangle of life-threads. In this case, the bewildering strands of a broken marriage are laced with excruciating pain. The author, stripped of her dignity and possessions, struggles to hang on to her thin shred of faith in God.

Through her story, the author explains how she nurtured her weak faith into a strong, joyful confidence in God. She describes the slow, sometimes obscure "needlework" of God until she can see the gorgeous tapestry of her life on the other side wrought through the inexplicable devastation of her marriage.

The tapestry in this story, however, did not happen automatically. Each ordering of the pattern was a heart-wrenching lesson that could not be learned without suffering. The author will lead you to understand these hard lessons of rejection, humiliation, absolute surrender, forgiveness, chastening, and suffering trust in God.

In the end, the choice will be yours. Will you succumb to bitterness and unbelief toward your offenders, with the ugly tangles of your life left unsightly, even on the other side? Or will you choose to forgive your offenders and trust the suffering God allows as He weaves your character into a magnificent tapestry? May this story inspire you to make the better choice.

—John D. Martin

chapter one

Cast Down

Save me, O my God. The floods have risen.
Deeper and deeper I sink in the mire;
the waters rise around me.
I have wept until I am exhausted;
my throat is dry and hoarse;
my eyes are swollen with weeping,
waiting on my God to act.
(Psalm 69:1- 3, The Living Bible).

This verse describes how I felt as my marriage collapsed. Many women have been rejected and traded for other models by men who vowed to love and cherish them for better or for worse, in health and in sickness, until death parted them.

In marriage, God Himself binds together the man and woman as one flesh for life. When the two are pried apart and the marriage is broken, the break is jagged and torn, unable to heal properly. Each new encounter with the unfaithful spouse exposes the wound, still raw and bleeding.

This whole experience has been a soul-searching process for me. Before my marriage, I thought if my husband and I had problems in our relationship, we would work through them peacefully. I dearly loved (and still love) my handsome, talented husband, and I believed separation from him would be a disgrace to God's name. Also, I didn't want to see our family broken apart. After I knew our marriage was not what it should be, I often prayed earnestly, "No matter what I need to endure, please, Lord, never let us separate."

I firmly believe God's directives for the wife who faces the challenges of a marriage that is less than ideal:

> And unto the married I [Paul] command, yet not I, but the Lord, let not the wife depart from her husband: but and if she depart, let her remain unmarried, or be reconciled to her husband: and let not the husband put away his wife. But to the rest speak I, not the Lord: If any brother hath a wife that believeth not, and she be pleased to dwell with him, let him not put her away. And the woman which hath an husband that believeth not, and if he be pleased to dwell with her, let her not leave him. For the unbelieving husband is sanctified by the wife, and the unbelieving wife is sanctified by the husband: else were your children unclean; but now are they holy. But if the unbelieving depart, let him depart. A brother or a sister is not under bondage in such cases: but God has called us to peace (1 Corinthians 7:10-15).

I desperately wanted to follow the Apostle Paul's advice, and for many years before our separation, I prayed earnestly for our failing marriage. God answered many prayers, yet it seemed the more I prayed for our marriage, the worse the situation became. I felt that God did not care enough to answer, yet I prayed on, knowing He could do the impossible.

However, after thirty-one years of marriage, we separated.

chapter two

Cast Out

February 9, 1992, I awoke at three a.m. to hear my husband tell me I needed to find somewhere else to live. He would no longer permit me to live at home. He was entirely serious, and it was impossible to reason with him. Crushed but mercifully numb, I went upstairs and just sat for several hours, unable to function. I couldn't pray except to groan, "My God, my God." Surely he was not serious! If only I could cry, I thought maybe that would release this crushing weight gnawing at the pit of my stomach.

Where could I go? What could I do? I wanted to disappear, but my concern for my family ruled that out—my family, how could I break the tragic news to our children? Four of our seven children still lived at home, although they were adults. James, our married son, lived nearby, and two children lived out of the community.

Finally, I decided to go back downstairs where my husband was fast asleep. How could he sleep after putting my life into such a spin? For me, all thought of sleep was gone, yet I crawled back into bed with him until it was time to get up and face the day.

I couldn't force myself to relay the message to the children. It seemed cruel to put them through more grief and tumult. But ten hours later, I knew I could not put it off any longer. I called the children, telling them to meet me at my son's house that afternoon.

My children's bottled emotions took over as we tried to decide what steps we needed to take. I was still in shock.

I called our bishop for advice. He recommended that under the circumstances, I probably should leave since my husband had told me to do so. He also advised that the children should leave with me. In the end, however, I gave them the choice to stay or to go.

We decided to move in temporarily with James and Joanna and their six-month-old son Jeffery. Then we went back home, and I cooked my husband's favorite meal: hamburgers, macaroni, and corn. This was the last meal we ate together. As the girls washed the dishes and cleaned up, I tried once more to reason with him, but I told him that if he hadn't changed his mind, we would leave yet that evening. A dark look crossed his face as he grabbed his hat and left the house.

I walked through the house with tormented groans, sometimes doubling over in agony and crying, "Oh, God, I can't, I can't leave! What do I take? What do I leave?"

I took only my clothes, my quilt frame, and four hundred dollars I had been paid for a quilt I had just sold. While the children loaded their belongings onto the pickup, I still had hopes that my husband would change his mind and tell me I could stay. Maybe he would follow us as we left, telling us we could return. But he didn't, and we learned that day something of what it means to dwell in this world as strangers and pilgrims.

We had no home and few earthly possessions on that memorable night as we left the man I had promised to stand by through thick and thin. In leaving, how could I keep that solemn promise I had made to God before men? I wanted to obey and honor God in all that I did, but I saw no honorable way to stay in this situation. I could not see how anything good would ever come from this. My husband had given me no choice.

A profound despair settled over me. David the Psalmist graphically described what I experienced when he begged God to lift him from the miry clay and the pit. "I am poor and needy," David confesses in Psalm 40:17, "yet the Lord thinketh upon me: thou art my help and my deliverer; make no tarrying, O my God." Did the Lord "think on me" too? I told God that if this separation lasted for a year, I would never make it: the miry clay would surely overtake me. My heart was shattered into hundreds of pieces as I lay in bed at James's house that night, sorting through the fog in my mind.

As I write, it has been fifteen years since that night, and I don't know where my husband is. In another Psalm, we hear David confess:

> The sacrifices of God are a broken spirit: a broken and a contrite heart, O God, thou wilt not despise (Psalm 51:17).

Although I did not know how God could approve of my life, I believe He saw my crushed heart, and this He did not despise.

"Time heals," they say, and in some ways it does, even though the pain probably will never go away. As I look back over the winding, rocky path I have walked, it is easier to see the big picture. I am able now to see some things I could not see before. These are the lessons I wish to share.

chapter three

Searching for Answers

A fter six years of a good marriage, our relationship had begun going downhill by spells. We still experienced many good times, but the situation gradually became worse. In desperation I started reading all the marriage books I could find.

I had prayed for years that God would show me where I was wrong and where I could improve our marriage. But now I often went on guilt trips, blaming myself when things did not go well. Now I had more questions than answers. Had I not prayed right, or had I prayed with wrong motives? In spite of all my analyzing, I could not seem to lay my finger on the problem, nor could I cope with my misery.

The very thing that I had so earnestly prayed would never happen, had happened. Many women might have turned to alcohol or drugs to drown out the pain, but I was a Christian, so I could not do those things. What then could I do to relieve the awful, gnawing emotional pain eating at me like a cancer? All these questions and the pain of rejection drove me to my knees. Answers were sometimes slow in coming, but bit by bit, God gently taught me lessons.

One evening I came across a verse that gave me hope and focus. God's words before me said, "Therefore remove sorrow from thy heart, and put away evil from thy flesh" (Ecclesiastes 11:10). "Yes, Lord," I replied. "I truly want to, but how do I remove sorrow from my heart when things are going from bad to worse?"

His answer was clear: I could not change my husband, but I could work on improving myself and my relationship with my Lord. God was not asking me to be responsible for my husband's actions. It was a tall enough order to be responsible for my own choices.

The fact that I had found something I could do excited me. I could focus on my own attitudes and reactions to circumstances regardless of what my husband did. More important, I needed to deepen my relationship with God. I had a goal, and I searched my heart for pride, resentment, bitterness, jealousy, and discouragement. I looked for anything that marred my relationship with my heavenly Father.

chapter four

The "Who Am I" Question

Pride wears several guises. Sometimes it convinces us that we are better, more deserving, more worthy than those around us. At other times, pride convinces us that we are nothing. Both of these beliefs are lies.

Jesus' words are sometimes surprising: "Woe unto you, when all men shall speak well of you" (Luke 6:26). Why was I so afraid of what other people thought of me? Pride caused my feelings to be hurt when people did not think and speak well of me. I realized this hurt was a sly way for pride to get a foothold.

I had to stop wondering what others were thinking. They had never walked in my shoes, and I hoped they never would. God required me only to do my best regardless of how it looked to someone else. For "they measuring themselves by themselves, and comparing themselves among themselves, are not wise" (2 Corinthians 10:12). Comparing myself to those around me was making me feel worthless. I was yielding to Satan's lies.

When my husband's unexpected explosions of anger and accusations sent me reeling, my response was not to yell or fight back. Instead, I became hurt and crushed to the point that I could not respond properly; I was afraid I would do or say something I would forever regret. When I harbored negative feelings or thoughts, I would react improperly at the most unexpected moments.

How could I gain victory over all my negative thoughts? I found an important key in Philippians 4:8:

Finally, brethren, whatsoever things are true, whatsoever things are honest, whatsoever things are just, whatsoever things are pure, whatsoever things are lovely, whatsoever things are of good report; if there be any virtue, and if there be any praise, think on these things.

As I think on these things, there is no room for the negative thoughts Satan delights to inject into my mind. As I put my mind under the authority of Jesus and kept it pure by replacing the bad thoughts with good thoughts, I could gain victory.

God had clearly shown me that He expected only for me to do my best. He would see to the rest. That sounded so simple, yet I found it hard not to worry. What if my responses hindered my husband from coming back to me?

No matter how many regrets I had and how often I wished I had done something differently, what was done was done. When I confessed to God, He cleansed and removed my sin as far as the east is from the west. Praise God! I didn't have to keep beating myself for my failures. By myself I could not change my thought patterns. It took both willpower and God's grace. I can testify that God's grace is sufficient to keep our hearts and minds pure and holy, free from anger and bitterness.

Because my feelings so often cannot be trusted, I need to embrace the facts and remind myself of who I am in

Christ. In Him I am worth as much as the most beloved wife.
Here are the facts I choose to believe:

- I have been accepted by Christ; I am His child. "But as many as received him, to them gave he power to become the sons of God, even to them that believe on his name" (John 1:12).
- I am His friend. "Henceforth I call you not servants; for the servant knoweth not what his lord doeth: but I have called you friends; for all things that I have heard of my Father I have made known unto you" (John 15:15).
- He bought me with a great price. "For ye are bought with a price: therefore glorify God in your body, and in your spirit, which are God's" (1 Corinthians 6:20).
- I belong to Him and am a member of His body. I am called a saint. "Unto the church of God which is at Corinth, to them that are sanctified in Christ Jesus, called to be saints, with all that in every place call upon the name of Jesus Christ our Lord, both theirs and ours" (I Corinthians 1:2).
- I have been justified. My slate is clean. "Being justified freely by his grace through the redemption that is in Christ Jesus" (Romans 3:24).
- I have been received as God's child and have access to God through the Holy Spirit. "For through him we both have access by one Spirit unto the Father" (Ephesians 2:18).
- I have been redeemed and forgiven of all my sins. "In whom we have redemption through his blood, even the forgiveness of sins" (Colossians 1:14).
- I am complete in Christ. "And ye are complete in him, which is the head of all principality and power" (Colossians 2:10).

- I am God's workmanship. "For we are his workman ship, created in Christ Jesus unto good works, which God hath before ordained that we should walk in them" (Ephesians 2:10).

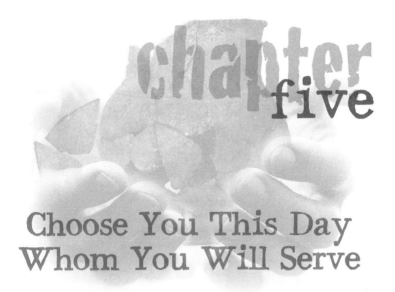

chapter five

Choose You This Day Whom You Will Serve

I learned the hard way that separations usually leave touchy, tender spots—potential holes in a wife's defenses where Satan can invade and build strongholds without the woman realizing what is happening. An unfaithful spouse can trigger nasty, undesirable reactions. Normally easygoing people lose their calm, responding in anger, nagging, hate, revenge, bitterness, and jealousy. When the protective umbrella of spiritual authority God gives to shield wives from Satan's attacks is gone, they are left open and vulnerable to Satan's attacks.

It is the easiest thing in the world to cover up our responses with excuses: "I can't help it. I've been hurt so badly." But no woman can blame her spouse for actions that are ultimately her responsibility. We choose how we will respond, and our responses do matter. When I point a finger at someone, three are pointing back at me. God says, "Why beholdest thou the mote [wrongdoing] that is in thy brother's [husband's] eye [life], but considerest not the beam that is in thine own eye [life]?" (Matthew 7:3).

As I walked through my valley of sorrow, I came to the same crossroad many times. Did I want to walk the road of revenge, hate, anger, and bitterness, or would I take the other road?

When our tormentors get a taste of their own medicine, our human nature wants to celebrate, but God says:

> Rejoice not when thine enemy falleth, and let not thine heart be glad when he stumbleth: lest the LORD see it, and it displease him, and he turn away his wrath from him (Proverbs 24:17, 18).

Do not take revenge, my friends, but leave room for God's wrath, for it is written: "It is mine to avenge; I will repay," says the Lord. On the contrary: "If your enemy is hungry, feed him; if he is thirsty, give him something to drink. In doing this, you will heap burning coals on his head." Do not be overcome by evil, but overcome evil with good (Romans 12:19-21, NIV).

Ye have heard that it hath been said, Thou shalt love thy neighbor, and hate thine enemy. But I say unto you, Love your enemies, bless them that curse you, do good to them that hate you, and pray for them which despitefully use you, and persecute you; That ye may be the children of your Father which is in heaven: for he maketh his sun to rise on the evil and on the good, and sendeth rain on the just and on the unjust. For if ye love them which love you, what reward have ye? (Matthew 5:43-46).

God does not ask the Christian to be sure the "enemy" gets what he deserves; God asks instead that His children commit everything to the righteous Judge and pray for those who treat us with spite. It is hard to be angry with a person for whom we are regularly praying. In fact, our suffering can lead us to love in ways we never knew were possible.

This then is where the two roads lead: one is the way to becoming an angry, resentful woman, the other is the way to becoming a soft-hearted woman of love and mercy. I am still on the path, still coming to crossroads, but I know which way I want to follow.

Forgiveness might not look like an easy path, but the way of bitterness is deceptively treacherous, and God warns us in Hebrews 12:15 of its potential devastation, saying, "Looking diligently . . . lest any root of bitterness springing up trouble you, and thereby many be defiled."

Bitterness is an enemy not readily recognizable, and many who have experienced hurt like I have mistakenly called it deep hurt or disappointment. Its beginning is often subtle, and when not overcome, bitterness brings a host of problems. Emotional stress drains energy from our bodies in the same way a physical problem can. Before we know it, the offender starts to control our lives. As we become so engrossed with the offenses and the offender, that person soon affects all our thoughts, goals, and attitudes until we become like the person who wronged us.

Harboring bitter thoughts is a direct violation of Scripture.

Whatsoever things are true, whatsoever things are honest, whatsoever things are just, whatsoever things are pure, whatsoever things are lovely, whatsoever things are of good report; if there be any virtue, and if there be any praise, think on these things (Philippians 4:8).

Not only did I find myself harboring bitterness against my husband, but I also found myself subconsciously blaming God for my circumstances. I thought, "He could change this. He could have kept it from happening. If He has the power, why doesn't He do something?" Thoughts such as these can easily evolve into anger and bitterness toward God Himself.

When I recognized my bitterness toward God, I asked Him to help me overcome these negative thoughts. One of the hardest things of all was to learn to trust Him. I chose to respond to God's time-proven promise:

> Trust in the Lord with all thine heart; and lean not unto thine own understanding. In all thy ways acknowledge him, and he shall direct thy paths (Proverbs 3:5, 6).

Many times I fought the power of darkness, which threatened to drag me down. I learned to say along with Job, "Shall we receive good at the hand of God, and shall we not receive evil?" (Job 2:10).

Negative feelings can cause chronic anxiety, serious depression, general mistrust, anger, resentment, and hatred. Refusing to forgive has even worse consequences. If we don't forgive, neither will our heavenly Father forgive us.

Matthew 18 gives the account of a servant who owed the king ten thousand talents and couldn't pay it. When the servant fell at the king's feet begging for mercy, the king had compassion and forgave all the debt.

The servant who had been pardoned then went out and found a man who owed him the small sum of a hundred pence. He put his hands to the debtor's throat and demanded full payment. The man begged for mercy, but the man who had just been released by the king would not hear of it. He cast his fellow servant into prison until he would pay it all.

When the king learned what had happened, he was furious and delivered the unforgiving lender to the tormentors until he could pay all he owed the king. It was a high price to pay for refusing to show mercy. "So likewise shall my heavenly Father do also unto you," Jesus said, "if ye from your hearts forgive not every one his brother their trespasses" (Matthew 18:35).

Physicians have connected bitterness to physical responses such as accelerated heart rate, high blood pressure and cholesterol, and a weakened immune system, which makes the body more vulnerable to diseases, including cancer. The way of bitterness is a hard way.

The unforgiving spirit might come in the back door, as I well know. A young woman who thought she had forgiven everyone still felt many symptoms that come with bitterness. She finally came to her wits' end. She could think of no one left to forgive.

The counselor asked her, "Have you forgiven yourself? You have forgiven everyone else."

The woman's eyes filled with tears and she said, "I don't think I will ever be able to."

I had not realized that when I beat up myself for things I had already asked God to forgive, I am essentially saying the blood of Jesus is not powerful enough to take away my sins. Doubt and unbelief have no place in the Christian's life. Jesus opened the prison doors of our hearts, and it is up to us to walk out in freedom.

chapter six

Giving Up

"Giving up" sounds like an admission of defeat, and certainly God does not call anyone to a life of defeat. God does, however, call us to offer our most precious possessions on an altar of devotion. Sometimes He gives it back; sometimes He doesn't. God asked Abraham to sacrifice his only beloved son on the altar, and Genesis 22 records that he obeyed. When God saw Abraham's obedience, He sent a ram to be offered instead.

Giving up my right to my husband was a struggle for many years before we separated. During these struggles, one evening stands out vividly in my memory. It was one of many spiritual battles that raged in my heart. I learned that some of the most difficult battles are not fought on battlefields of war, but in the hearts of people.

I knew where my husband was going that night when he left the house, and the spirit of jealousy raged through my heart. My pain mixed with anger, and I thought, "If I could get hold of him, I'd show him a thing or two." After he left, I went to my bedroom and fell on my knees. I could not pray. All I could do was utter, "Oh, my God, please." I cried in utter desperation and anger until I could not cry anymore. It seemed as though my unspoken prayer went only to the ceiling.

Finally my spirit calmed, and the Holy Spirit whispered, "My child, you will never be happy feeling like this." The battle raged with a violence that tore my heart. One minute I would think I had given up my husband. The next instant I would latch onto him for fear of losing him. I pleaded, "Oh, Lord, I can't. He's mine, not someone else's. I can't give him up!"

How could God ask me to give up all my cherished dreams of a happy Christian home? I was not praying for something wrong or against God's will! After what seemed like hours, I gave up to God all the rights I had to my husband. I could now truly say, "Not my will but thine be done."

I remembered the battle Jesus had waged in the garden to say those words. He had followed through with his promise and He died a terrible death. I was not being literally crucified. I had only entered into His suffering.

Although my heart was being torn to shreds, I prayed, "Lord, I give him to you. If I lose him, I lose him. I want Your will. Lord, hold me tight. Don't let me slip. I know that whatever happens, You will go before me and help me bear the load."

I smile to remember that when my husband came back on that occasion, I was so glad to see him. I forgot all about being angry. Somehow, God's grace eased the anger and replaced it with mercy in what can only be a miracle.

chapter seven

Battle Won,
But the War Goes On

O nce I experienced victory on that memorable night, I found relief. A battle had been won, but the war raged on. There were other battles as I constantly faced new situations.

After we left home, the little contact I had with my husband occurred when I would pass the farm where we had lived. If I was fortunate, I might get a glimpse of him going about his work on the farm. I sometimes would pass him on the road. These contacts always left me breathless. Here was my own husband to whom I had promised my very life. How I longed to sit down and talk with him and work through our differences! If only my husband would have given me a wave or a smile, or even just a look of recognition, my heart would have sung for joy.

But that never happened, and I was left each time feeling helpless and utterly defeated. I had lost my identity. As much as I wanted to see my husband, each encounter sent me into another emotional spin, with another battle to work through.

My heart cried out, "Oh, my God, why has he so utterly forsaken me? I feel that even You must be doing the same. Why does it seem that there is just no hope?"

Many a night after seeing him, I would weep and pray well into the morning hours, pleading for mercy for him, for me, for our family, and for our marriage. Where was God? My heart cried, "Forsake me not, O LORD: O my God, be not far from me" (Psalm 38:21).

When I opened my Bible, I often asked God to show me a chapter or a verse that would give me the grace and strength to get through this battle once again. I found many Scripture verses to claim and cherish. Reading through the Psalms and embracing the truths in them often brought a healing balm, partially restoring sleep and peace. The Bible was my source of comfort—sometimes the only one.

Instead of denying or fighting the pain, I found that embracing, acknowledging, and accepting the deep emotional pain squarely helped me bear it. Letting God do His perfect work in the midst of the pain brought a healing balm.

However, healing for an unresolved marital separation is ongoing until death. God plainly says, "Wherefore they are no more twain, but one flesh. What therefore God hath joined together, let not man put asunder" (Matthew 19:6). Only death can bring an end to the reality of a broken marriage.

In pastures green? Not always.
Sometimes He Who knows best,
In kindness leads me.
In weary ways, where heavy shadows be,
So when on the hilltops high and fair,
I dwell, or in the sunless valley where,
The shadows lie, what matters, He is there.
　　　　　　　　　　　　　　　—Berry
From *Streams in the Desert*

When we are tempted to question God's gentle leading, He remembers, and not one step will He ask us to take, that we are not able to endure. If we dread the next step, that seems to be coming, either He will strengthen us, or halt it that we need not go through it. We can trust Him. He will go on before us, holding us and guiding us so we won't slip (*Streams in the Desert*).

God's Word says:

There hath no temptation taken you but such as is common to man: but God is faithful, who will not suffer you to be tempted above that ye are able; but will with the temptation also make a way to escape, that ye may be able to bear it (1 Corinthians 10:13).

That is a promise!

eight

Treasures

I struggled to lay down my personal "right" to earthly possessions. This was another gift God was calling me to lay on the altar, but in the light of losing my husband, the possessions mattered little. We had a joint deed to the farm. Two years after our separation, my husband called me and asked if I would sign off on the deed so he could sell the farm.

I told him I needed some time to think about it. Some concerned people advised me to refuse if my husband did not promise to give me what was legally mine. I certainly did not want to sign off. I knew I would be losing most of the material things I owned. But what decision would speak most clearly to my husband? What would my decision tell him about me and my love for him? Which choice would best reflect the redemptive nature of the God I longed for him to find again?

While searching the Scripture and pleading with God for guidance, my eyes fell on Jesus' words in Matthew 5:38-48. "If a man took my cloak, I was to also offer him my coat" (paraphrase). I could find no excuse to fight for my rights. I sensed Jesus clearly directing me to commit the injustice of it all to Him, the righteous Judge. Our earthly possessions belonged to Him. If God wanted me to have my share, He would lay it on my husband's heart to provide it. If my husband did not change his mind, God Himself would be my provider. I just needed to trust Him.

Several other passages, especially Hebrews 10:34, 35 and 1 Peter 2 and 3, seemed written for me. I did not get any money, yet I was exceedingly rich compared to my husband. He might have had most of our earthly possessions, but I had the treasures that mattered in eternity. They could not be destroyed by moths, rust, or thieves. I had all the children. They had chosen to go with me. I had my God, which no man could take from me. I had a clear conscience toward God and toward other people, instead of a nagging conscience accusing me.

We met at the courthouse to sign the deed. As we sat there in front of the lawyer, whom we both knew, it felt so natural, so complete and whole. Oh, just to forget the past with all its struggles and go on in peace.

Several days later, my husband called, wondering whether I would be at home if he came to have me endorse the check, which was made out to both of us. He had never been at the house where I now lived, and I was nervous. I quickly breathed a prayer for protection and guidance. My husband lived only two miles away, and he soon appeared at the door. He handed me the check, told me where to sign, and was gone. Gone. Gone! He soon moved into a house even closer to us, but I seldom saw him.

Was I being a doormat by signing off the deed and letting him have it all? I had to think of Jesus, the perfect example of one who pleased God. Although He owned everything, He did not demand even a place to lay His head.

The church and the community showered us with food and household items. They provided all we needed to start over with housekeeping. It was somewhat humiliating to accept so many handouts. After all, it was not their responsibility, and one could argue that I had made the decision to give everything to my husband.

Giving is often much easier than receiving. I suppose someone must be at the receiving end, or there would be no one to receive the gift of the giver. But why me? As much as it humbled me, my heart sang with gratitude and praise as I felt the care and love from those around me. Truly the Lord took; then He gave and gave through His beloved people.

One day when we were at my son's house processing corn, one of the boys came home and said, "Dad is moving out of state, but he did not say where." My heart sank "to the bottom of my feet." For the rest of the day I was in a daze, my heart filled with tumult. I cried out, "Oh, God, please don't let him leave! What if I never see him again?"

I desperately needed to be alone to work through this with God. My hopes for reconciliation were shattered. It was dark when I left James's house. I drove past the house where my husband was living. Everything was dark.

I drove home, barely able to see the road through my tears. I entered my blessed home, where there was no one to hear me cry. Throwing myself on the bed, I wept till I could weep no more. I thought I would never stop crying. My precious husband was gone!

"Anyway," I told myself, "he will be my husband as long as I live, no matter how many other women he marries." It was the covenant we had made before God and men.

Once more I picked up my precious Bible and found the comfort to keep on. I read,

> Why art thou cast down, O my soul? And why art thou disquieted within me? Hope thou in God: for I shall yet praise him, who is the health of my countenance, and my God (Psalm 42:11).

"Hope thou in God!" What more could I do? Since that day when my husband moved out of the state, no family member has talked to him nor seen him. We do not know where he is.

I wondered if I should get a job. The children objected to this. They said they would rather support me. They wanted to come home to a mom and not an empty house after a day's work. Especially now that they were fatherless, they needed the support and sense of family and home that I could give them.

I felt I needed to honor the children's request. As I now see them all serving the Lord, I am richly blessed and rewarded for any sacrifices I made. The children have done a wonderful job supporting me financially and physically, and the Lord has richly blessed them.

Some time later, I told my son that after the children no longer needed me, I'd like to work in a store. Overhearing me, my four-year-old granddaughter said, "But, Grandma, I might need you all the time." That settled it in my heart. What greater calling and influence can anyone have for good? "The hand that rocks the cradle rules the world." I am not rocking cradles anymore, but my home is still a home for my family. Jesus said in Matthew 6:21, "Where your treasure is, there will your heart be also." My family is a treasure of inestimable worth.

chapter nine

Building Both Faith and a House

E ven if the real treasures are stored above, physical needs still exist. Moving four times within five months certainly helped to develop my trust and faith in God. After much prayer and advice from fellow Christians, we bought a lot where we hoped to build a house. But how could we build with no money? While struggling with the issue one night, I told the Lord that if He wanted us to build a house, He would have to build it. This seemed a too-literal application of "except the LORD build the house, they labour in vain that build it" (Psalm 127:1).

After I handed the house-building over to God by faith, things started to happen. He sent a good carpenter who offered to build our house working with volunteers from the community. A brother-in-law took charge of much of the paperwork and generally making things happen on our thorn patch of a lot. Friends loaned money without charging interest and made donations. Two months from the time the foundation was dug, we moved into a completed house.

Our hearts were filled to overflowing as we saw how God was meeting our needs. This built our trust in Him in a new way. The children pitched in and helped pay the debt of building our house. As our needs were met, we received the much-needed assurance that God had not forsaken us.

chapter ten

Rejection and Loneliness

Rejection and all the worthless feelings that go with it were hard for me to handle. The night I sat up in bed and heard my husband say, "You need to find somewhere else to live; you can't stay here," were words that hit me so hard I went numb. I lost all confidence that I could do anything right. I felt worthless, like a piece of junk ready to be discarded. I blamed myself for the failure of our marriage.

Facing people was very difficult. I thought I simply could not do it. But I knew the longer I waited, the harder it would become. I was sure people thought I must be a terrible woman if even my husband could not stand being around me. When I finally did get up the courage to go somewhere, I wanted to hide in a corner. An unfaithful spouse destroys all sense of worth.

Now, years later, I still cringe when non-Christians know I am separated from my husband. It is a disgrace to God's name and a bad example. We should have been able to work this out.

I discovered that I felt better as I poured my life into other people. Babysitting and foster care became avenues that allowed love to flow through my heart again. After five years, our last child married. Also, I stopped babysitting two little girls who had become so much a part of me. I again felt alone and deserted. All I wanted to do was to sit in the rocker and cry.

Often I wept in my moments alone. Grief overwhelmed my soul. A counselor later told me, "The very fact that you could cry was the reason you made it through." Tears are no disgrace. Releasing them to God can bring relief and cleansing. Tears mellow our hearts, while suppressing tears hardens our hearts.

chapter eleven

Walking With Jesus

A s easy as it would have been to indulge in self pity, bitterness, and revenge, there was a better way. Jesus asked me to embrace the way of peace, and I continue to choose the way Jesus taught. I have never regretted it.

I have found I can trust my Jesus. Together, Jesus and I are traveling homeward. He leads me by the hand and carries me through the valleys.

Many times I had to tell myself to focus only on the present, to live it to the fullest, to remember that it would never come back. When I looked to the days ahead, I sank into despair. I had to focus on my heavenly Father and not on my seemingly impossible circumstances. God wanted to fill the vacancy I felt because of my husband's absence, but I also needed someone with flesh and blood with whom I could talk and share. I was afraid to trust anyone with my inner struggles, and this loneliness drove me closer to my God.

The times I spent sitting at the feet of Jesus were important, even when I did not feel like taking it. When I did not spend the time alone with God, my spiritual life soon withered. I learned that my time with God was essential if I was to live above survival mode. Sometimes I could not find the words to pray or to keep my focus on what I was reading in the Bible; I could only come before Him with groans and heart cries, yet God heard and understood.

Someone said, "When you get to the foot of the mountain, don't stop, but climb to higher height." We can climb to a higher spiritual ground than we ever dreamed possible. Each mountain we face becomes an opportunity to rise higher. Looking back, we can marvel at God's grace and guidance.

So often I forced myself to go on when all I wanted to do was sit at the bottom and cry, "I can't." Jesus had walked the path before me, and I determined to follow close in His footsteps. Only in Him could my aching void be filled. Jesus wanted to bring beauty out of ashes and joy out of mourning. So I needed to let Him fill me with joy that overflows, despite the circumstances. I could delight in joy again, even if it was bittersweet.

I can say honestly that God's love has shone through the haze, and I can wholeheartedly thank and praise my precious Redeemer for keeping His promises. I have long cherished John 14. Jesus promised to give me a comforter. I have experienced that comfort not only through His work in my heart but also through my children and the church. They are His people who brought words of encouragement, food, and other gestures of love and service.

chapter twelve

In Everything Give Thanks

Instead of looking at my blessings, many were the days I let myself focus on all the unfairness I felt life had handed me. I told myself that I had a right to pity myself, but wallowing in the fact that life isn't fair was getting me nowhere. God gave some verses that helped me through a time of particularly dark despondency. Here are a couple of them.

[Being] rooted and built up in him [Jesus], and stablished in the faith, as ye have been taught, abounding therein with thanksgiving (Colossians 2:7).

Giving thanks always for all things [or in all things], unto God and the Father in the name of our Lord Jesus Christ (Ephesians 5:20).

Being thankful in undesirable situations does not come naturally. I felt more like yelling, raging, blaming, or giving in to discouragement. It was impossible for me in my own strength to rejoice in suffering, but with God all things are possible. This needed my constant attention, especially when I was receiving nothing but criticism from my husband.

I realized that discouragement was one of the devil's most effective tools to destroy me. It was a load of baggage I could not afford to carry along on my journey. But how could I be truly thankful? I learned that it was a matter of my will and God's grace. God was in control, and He allows nothing that cannot be turned into something beautiful. He is a master craftsman shaping a vessel for His glory.

> But now, O LORD, thou art our Father; we are the clay, and thou our potter; and we are all the work of thy hand (Isaiah 64:8).

Just as the clay cannot shape itself, so we too are dependent on God to turn us into something beautiful and useful. He shapes away the rough edges to make His children fit for His use. Because we are special to Him, He takes great pains to make us into what He wants us to be. He looks beyond our present circumstances to the finished product, and that is why we can thank Him.

Thanking God in all circumstances does not mean we are thanking Him for the wrongdoings, but for His overriding purpose in allowing it to happen and for the shaping and crafting He artfully works in our lives. God is never responsible for anyone's wrongdoings, but He is able to use the wrong actions of another to further His purposes.

If wicked men had not crucified Jesus, no salvation could have been provided for us. Of course, they had to bear the consequences of their own actions, despite the wonderful result.

True gratefulness turns negative thoughts into praise, for bitterness and unhappiness cannot exist in a thankful heart. In the name of our Lord Jesus Christ, I needed to cast out the junk in my mind threatening to drag me down. I saw its potential to eat like a cancer without a cure. Thank God, however, this cancer has a cure: the Lord Jesus Christ. As I focused on His greatness, His love, and His faithfulness, He helped me focus my thoughts on something besides myself and my suffering.

thirteen

Suffering With Jesus

The Scriptures have a lot to say about suffering for righteousness' sake and even rejoicing in suffering. Peter wrote, "If any man suffer as a Christian, let him not be ashamed; but let him glorify God on this behalf" (1 Peter 4:16). Who feels like rejoicing after being misused? A wise lady once pointed me to a truth in 1 Peter 2 and 3. I had never before connected the chapters, but I saw it plainly now. The words "likewise ye wives" in chapter 3 meant chapter 2 also was talking to a woman like me. To make it practical, I put myself into the verses:

> For this is thankworthy, if [I] for conscience toward God endure grief, suffering wrongfully. For what glory is it, if, when [I am] buffeted for [my] faults, [I] shall take it patiently? but if, when [I] do [the best I know how], and [still] suffer for it, [I] take it patiently, this is acceptable with God (1 Peter 2:19, 20).

I noticed the word "patiently" in verses 19 and 20. Patience is very difficult when it seems that things are getting out of hand. Nevertheless, Someone had pioneered this path before me, blazing a trail for me to follow.

> For even hereunto were ye called: because
> Christ also suffered for us, leaving us an example,
> that ye should follow his steps. Who did no sin,
> neither was guile found in his mouth (1 Peter 2:
> 21, 22, emphasis added).

According to verse 23, when Jesus was reviled or accused of something, He did not retaliate. Often my first response to any accusation was to react. How easy it was to utter piercing words that broke and wounded those I loved and cared for the most! However, that was not Jesus' response, and it should not be mine. No evil words came from His lips despite the most undeserved, gruesome treatment.

Chapter 3 makes Christ's example poignantly practical: "Likewise, ye wives, be in subjection to your own husbands." Likewise! What does this mean but that we wives are to respond to our own husbands in the same way Jesus did to His accusers, even when we are physically or verbally abused? He was our perfect example to follow, and we are told to do as He did.

Chapter 2 says of Christ, "Who his own self bare our sins in his own body on the tree, . . . by whose stripes ye were healed." He did this so I could go free. Now it is possible for His children to enter into His sufferings.

> Beloved, think it not strange concerning the
> fiery trial which is to try you, as though some
> strange thing happened unto you: but rejoice
> inasmuch as ye are partakers of Christ's sufferings
> (1 Peter 4:12, 13).

What does entering into Christ's suffering mean? Suffering with Christ is, in part, sharing the experience with Him. When we face rejection and pain as He did, and when we invite His presence with us during our suffering, we partake of or join together in Christ's suffering. He knows better than anyone else about the personal pain that overwhelms us in our darkest times.

As a rejected wife, I received comfort, reassurance, and direction from 1 Peter 3:1-18. Those who have suffered rejection can realize to a greater degree what Jesus suffered for us when He was rejected. It is harder for those who have not been in similar situations to understand and sympathize, but Jesus has been there and knows completely what we are going through. When we respond as Jesus responded to His heavenly Father, we are sharing in His suffering.

chapter
fourteen

God's Agent in Disguise

Is it true that God chose my offending husband as an agent to accomplish His particular purpose in me? This perspective might come to you as a surprise, but to me, it is a precious and deeply personal thought. All this heartache and struggle has a purpose, and I believe God has a plan to turn the ugliness into something beautiful. It is up to me to discover what God wants to accomplish in me today, whether or not I understand the larger picture.

The story of Joseph frequently comes to my mind. Genesis 37 describes how when he was seventeen years old, his brothers robbed him of the special coat of many colors their father had given him and threw him into a pit to die. Then they changed their minds, pulled him out, and sold him to the Ishmaelites instead.

In Egypt, he was bought by Potiphar, one of Pharaoh's officers, only to be falsely accused of attempting to molest Potiphar's wife. Potiphar then cast him into prison.

At age thirty Joseph was released from prison to interpret dreams for the king. The king made him overseer of all Egypt, where his foresight and management saved many people from starvation during seven years of famine.

Those saved from death included his brothers, who came to Egypt to buy corn that Joseph had stored up from seven plentiful years that preceded the famine. After he revealed himself to his brothers, he said, "So now it was not you that sent me hither, but God . . . but as for you, ye thought evil against me: but God meant it unto good" (Genesis 45:8; 50:20).

Joseph's story has many dark moments; the divine plan was hidden in a pit, behind prison bars, and in chains. In these times, he certainly could not have seen his bright future. Seeing how Joseph's life turned out to be God's way of saving people's lives has inspired love and compassion in me for struggling, hurting people.

As God provided for the needs of my family while living as strangers and pilgrims, my faith and trust in Him grew by leaps and bounds. Why did the props have to be knocked out from under me to teach me dependence and trust in my heavenly Father? Perhaps I was too independent and did not sufficiently see my need.

Now I wanted to be more grateful for the good memories of the years we had together instead of brooding over what I did not have. I went through the same grieving process as someone who has lost a loved one by death, only my experience was ongoing. I had to work through it again and again. Finally, I was able to say with Job:

> Naked came I out of my mother's womb, and naked shall I return thither; the LORD gave, and the LORD hath taken away; blessed be the name of the LORD (Job 1:21).

I came away from the broken home seminar at Penn Valley Christian Retreat in central Pennsylvania believing that maybe God did have a purpose for me. Recognizing a wise and loving heavenly Father working on my behalf kept me from becoming bitter.

That God wants to accomplish His purposes in us is the last thing on the minds of those of us who have experienced rejection. As we try to cope without the one on whom we depended most, contrary thoughts are overwhelming, threatening to pull us under. In the early stages of my experience, I scarcely got anything done beyond survival. I needed the confidence that God had special plans for me and that He could use every incident in my life for His glory. I am still enrolled in God's school, still learning.

In the name and power of Jesus and with His blood to cleanse our sins, normal, everyday women can overcome despite many circumstances that seem to the contary. The ability to cope comes from knowing and obeying God, not looking at the unfair knocks we receive in life. It takes God's grace working in us to live above these difficult situations, but it can be done.

chapter fifteen

What I Wish All Wives Knew

Praise

No marriage is easy to maintain, but the truth is that some people are almost impossible to live with. Some tools of the trade exist, though, that can make a difference in a marriage. I wish I had been more aware of these tools years ago.

Men thrive on honest admiration and words of affirmation. I do not know why it is so hard for women to praise their husbands for their strong points. (Yes, every man has them!) Waiting until they become the perfect husband to tell them what you appreciate about them is waiting until it is too late. It may take attention, humility, and willpower on your part, but it is worth it. Appreciate their efforts even if the work had not been done just as you would have wanted.

My husband is a gifted man, a jack of all trades. There is little he cannot do. His determination can accomplish a lot. What he does, he does right. He passed on these values to our sons. It does my heart good to see these traits in our children. God forbid that my husband ever got the idea that

I did not notice and appreciate his abilities and worth as a man.

Some men, however, find it hard to accept genuine love and words of affirmation. This baffled me. It seemed my husband wanted love, yet it was hard for him to accept it in the last years we lived together. Was I supposed to act as though I did not love him, or was I supposed to show love, even though it upset him? Learning the love language of one's husband is helpful. I now wonder if his love language was so different from mine that I just didn't know how to relate to him. Honestly, I still have not decided what my husband's love language was.

I heard one wife say she tries to find a positive trait in her husband, then draws her children's attention to it, even if it is as simple as being able to fry an egg better then she can. She was amazed how the children latched onto this attitude. It helped the children to hear something positive about their dad. After all, the wife is not the only one suffering when a marriage is failing; the children, too, are broken.

If children love their dad and hear nothing but negative criticism about him, it will not only destroy their regard for the one God has commanded them to love and respect, but it will also bring them pain to disdain the one they deeply wish to follow with admiration. As mothers and wives, often we are more responsible for the actions of our children than we realize.

A hurting wife once asked what she should do when she could not find anything for which to praise her husband. It is almost impossible to find something worthy of praise if we feed that negative attitude rather than the attitude of expecting something good. We can ask God to show us praiseworthy traits in our husbands. No one on this earth is without at least one good point, but much to Satan's delight, hurt often blinds us to the commendable traits our husbands do demonstrate.

If a husband hears nothing but nagging, criticism, and harsh words when he is at home, why would he be motivated to try to please his wife? Publicly shaming a husband or telling others of his mistakes will surely alienate him. On the other hand, hearing a kind, positive word from his wife or from his children, especially in public, can stir a man's heart in a positive way.

Contention

Solomon wrote about the contentious woman—the wife who argues, fusses, complains, and is never pleased. She is like a continual dripping of water from which there is no escape. Such a woman cannot be silenced anymore than an unwelcome wind can be locked away.

A continual dropping in a very rainy day and a contentious woman are alike. Whosoever hideth her hideth the wind (Proverbs 27:15, 16).

I have heard of prisoners forced to sit under constantly dripping water until it drove them insane. Do we drive our husbands insane by our contention?

"Contentious" means "being disagreeable, constantly arguing in a bossy way." I still need to evaluate myself to determine whether I am acting like a contentious, nagging, angry, hard-to-please woman. Answer these questions for yourself: What happens if the person who washes the dishes does a sloppy job? What if your husband or child hangs up laundry and pins a dress to the clothesline by the skirt instead of by the shoulder? What if someone's muddy shoes leave tracks on the floor? In response, what do you say or do?

Especially for the perfectionist, this can be a big deal, but for the sake of peace and harmony in the home, the godly woman learns to look past some mistakes and accepts the motive behind the other person's efforts. That consideration lasts for years.

I always cringe when I hear a woman responding contentiously to her husband. Why would a man want to please his wife if she criticizes everything he does? Women may be unaware of what they are doing, so the call to remain aware of our responses must be emphasized.

chapter

sixteen

Attitudes and Responses

Over time I have learned that a wife's response to her spouse in adverse situations can tip a delicate balance in her family. It determines how her children are going to respond to life, to their dad and mom, and to God. I saw my attitudes reflected in my children as I was being tested to the limit.

As I responded to a particular situation, I felt seven pairs of eyes looking straight through me. Inside I was crying, "Please do not look at me now."

On one occasion my teenage children and I were discussing a church problem. Later, overhearing them discussing the matter in stronger negative terms than I thought I had used, it hit me: They had gotten that attitude from none other than me. How could I expect them to become faithful, respectful church members if I degraded those in authority?

I apologized and told my teenagers we needed to pray for our church leaders instead of criticizing them, but unfortunately, our spoken words can never be retracted.

God's instruction to me was unquestionably plain: Respect and honor your husband despite the reasons you find not to do so. I needed to obey this command with a loving and willing heart, even though it was contrary to my human nature.

With a deep concern for my children's salvation, I went to the Lord in helpless despair in those earlier years when my husband told me one Sunday morning that he was not going to church anymore. "If these children turn out wrong, it is all your fault," he informed me.

Through Satan's temptation I came to believe it was useless to try raising my children for the Lord under the circumstances (then aged two to twelve). I nearly threw up my hands in defeat, but love for my children drove me on. I would fight the spiritual battles for them by example, by teaching, and by interceding in prayer. I told the Lord there was no way I could do it by myself; He would have to do it for me. He would have to take over. I believe He did what He promised He would do in Romans 8:26.

Likewise the Spirit also helpeth our infirmities: for we know not what we should pray for as we ought: but the Spirit itself maketh intercession for us with groanings which cannot be uttered.

As the old saying goes, hindsight is better than foresight. I often prayed desperately for God to improve the situation so the children would not become discouraged to the point of giving up following Him. Why was the Lord allowing it to become so difficult?

I realize now that God was using the difficult times to mold me into a more Christ-like image. I should have prayed not to be delivered from the trials, but to be taught by God as I allowed His Spirit to take control of my life. The easy life does not lead to greatness. I often told the children they were in God's own school of training.

A quote from *Streams in the Desert* explains it well:

When trouble comes, God will first adjust us to the trouble, and cause us to learn our lessons from it. His promise is, "I will be with Him in trouble; I will deliver Him and honor Him." But that will not come until we stop being restless and fretful about it and become calm and quiet.

At first we cry in anguish for deliverance from the pain of a broken heart. Only after we accept the brokenness and allow ourselves to feel the hurt do we, like Jesus, cry out, "Not my will, but Thy will be done. Help me learn what You want me to learn." Only then can peace come. God wants to do a purifying work in our hearts, leaving no room for anger or revenge. Peace does not come from getting what we want. Rather, it is the reward of a totally surrendered heart.

I now can say with certainty, "God is our refuge and strength, a very present help in trouble" (Psalm 46:1). Although I can now testify to this truth, for many years as the children were growing up, it seemed God had not heard my heart-rending cry for help in raising my children. During these difficult years, one message the Spirit made plain to me was that my children needed to love and respect their dad, and I needed to be their example. Years later, I realized God had given me this principle to follow, and that was why I had that strong urge to teach the children respect. It had been an answer to my prayer when I thought no answers were coming.

I clearly remember the day I realized that God had indeed answered my prayers. When I asked one of our now grown sons why he chose to become a Christian when he had many reasons to become hard and bitter, he said, "Mom, if you had not loved and respected Dad, but had instead criticized and run him down, I would never have become a Christian. I was waiting for you to say the wrong words to justify myself in going my own way."

After my son left, I broke down and cried with gratitude and praise. "Oh, Lord God, thank You for keeping me.

It was only You who kept me on the right track. Only You know how rough it has been and how often I felt all was lost. You not only heard my plea for help, but You led me and protected my children. How can I ever thank You enough?"

We might not see the results of our persevering faith until years later. We may have to sacrifice our own will and desires for the sake of our children, but it is worth it when we see them become Christians. As each of my children dedicated all to God and was baptized, I wept in thankfulness to the great I AM, Who alone made it possible.

Today my prayer for the children is that every difficult situation in their lives may become a steppingstone to higher ground.

God's wisdom cannot err,
His power cannot fail,
His love can never change,
To know that even His direct
Dealings are for our deepest spiritual gain.
Our troubles are only
Instruments for accomplishing His tender
And wise purposes for us.
See God in all things, great or small.
Give Him praise in whatever befalls.
                              —Author unknown

Jesus is our intercessor when words fail us, yet He also works powerfully through human intercessors. Frequently, when I felt I could not lift my head or feet anymore, my spirits would suddenly lift, and the world would look brighter again. Once more I could face the world and its problems. Someone must have prayed, and that person will never know the specific benefit of his prayer, but I know it made a difference. This message burns in my heart for mothers whose hearts are torn, bruised, and bleeding: When you feel you cannot go on any longer as you struggle alone to raise your precious children, take heart. God hears your prayers.

seventeen

Be at Peace

God gives us some hard commands, such as "Be at peace among yourselves" (1 Thessalonians 5:13) and "Follow peace with all men" (Hebrews 12:14). Follow peace with all men, even our worst enemies? How? Only by God's grace. Often have I asked God to fill me to overflowing with the unconditional love of Christ, a love I did not have of myself.

Romans 14:19 is the answer.

> Let us therefore follow after the things which make for peace, and things wherewith one may edify another.

Children get into fights because each insists on having his own way, and too many adults have never grown out of that stage. Even if a husband is selfish and ignores the wishes of his wife, she must answer for her own actions, not for her husband's.

What does it take to live peacefully with husbands who are misusing us? It means deferring to them, giving up our own will and desires to do things their way. We can state our wishes, but then yield to their decisions. Some may say this is becoming a doormat, but I believe it is following Jesus' example and actively pursuing peace.

Having two bosses in the home will not work, and God ordained men to be the leaders. Submitting can be hard for a wife when her leader is being unreasonable. But for the woman's peace and for the peace of her home, she needs to follow God's principles in all situations unless the husband's directive is contrary to God's Word. When the woman thus obeys, God will give her the needed grace.

Sin entered into the world by one single act of disobedience, causing Adam and Eve's expulsion from the Garden of Eden. Thus, much evil and tragedy entered the world which had been created perfect. It is God's command to obey all authority over us. Even when they are unreasonable, not doing so often leads to disaster.

Thankfully, my husband never demanded anything of me that went against God's commands. As unreasonable as he sometimes was, I could go along with what he asked of me. In my case, it was a matter of giving up what I might have called my personal rights.

chapter eighteen

Steps to Forgiveness

How oft shall my brother sin against me, and I forgive him? till seven times?' Jesus said unto him, I say not unto thee, Until seven times: but, until seventy times seven (Matthew 18:21, 22).

Forgiveness is necessary for healing the wounds left behind by emotional or physical trauma. The individual alone must make the choice to forgive.

As in every other area of our lives, Jesus is the perfect model for us. From the cross, He looked down on His enemies with pity and said, "Father, forgive them; for they know not what they do" (Luke 23:34). Jesus, our ultimate example, was wrongfully accused. Although His actions were perfect, He still suffered at the hands of others, and His message to us is unmistakable:

> But I say unto you, Love your enemies, bless them that curse you, do good to them that hate you, and pray for them which despitefully use you, and persecute you; that ye may be the children of your Father which is in heaven (Matthew 5:44,45).

You have the power either to forgive or to hold a grudge. Regardless of what gave rise to the unforgiveness, in order to be happy and free, you need to let go of the pains from the past to give and receive forgiveness. How does this miracle of forgiveness occur in our hearts? The following actions are key to forgiving:

- Acknowledge your hurt and anger. Too often we push the negative emotions down and cover them up, not acknowledging that we are hurt or angry. Hurt is very real, and God knows how you feel. But you need to tell Him about it for your own benefit.
- Realize that holding onto the pain only hurts your self. God wants to bear your pain with you, so you should cast it upon Him.
- Consciously and willingly let go of any need for revenge.
- Pray earnestly for the very ones who hurt you. Ask God to heal the wounds that caused them to hurt others.
- We forgive by releasing from accountability to us every person who has caused us pain. Pray that your own wounds do not lead you to wound others. We must ask God to help us to forget all the times we wish we had done differently. Much as we might wish to go back, we cannot relive or redo our past actions. What is done is done. Jesus has promised, "If we confess our sins, he is faithful and just to forgive us our sins, and to cleanse us from all unrighteousness" (1 John 1:9).

Bitterness, blame, and an unforgiving spirit are manifestations of hate, which is the same as murder in God's sight.

He that loveth not his brother [husband] abideth in death. Whosoever hateth his brother [husband] is a murderer: and ye know that no murderer hath eternal life abiding in him (1 John 3:14, 15).

By this standard, you may be murdering your spouse unconsciously in subtle ways. The following list may not seem so bad, yet they lead to hate and certainly do not cultivate love:

- Cutting him off and out of your life as though he did not exist.
- Thinking evil thoughts about him.
- Taking matters into your own hands instead of putting them into God's hand.
- Speaking unkindly to others about him.
- Wishing him harm, maybe even death, so you can go on with life.

The way to restore love in your heart for the man who has wronged you is to invest something good into his life, returning good for evil. Here are some ways to do this:

- Greet him with a smile.
- Praise him for his good qualities.
- Defend him to others in areas where you can.
- Express appreciation to him.
- Meet a basic need he has.
- Pray for him.

A primary characteristic of Christ-likeness is intercession, and God is teaching me how to intercede for my husband. Here are some thoughts I want to share with anyone who finds herself in a situation similar to mine:

How to pray for your husband:

- Confess to God any feelings you have for your husband good or bad.

- Make it a habit to admit to God that all your earthly ideals fall short of His heavenly wisdom. Ask Him to let you in on the reasons for this particular partnership at a time when He knows you are emotionally unfit to handle it.
- Make a list of your husband's good qualities and thank God for each one of them.
- Ask God to bless your husband richly—to prosper him, give him good health, and reward him with success. Ask God to make him the man He wants him to be.
- Pour out your heart to God. Tell Him what you need, where you hurt, and where you lack.
- Ask God to fulfill each of your requests in His way, in His time, through whomever He wishes and whenever He sees fit.
- Cry out asking God to give you a supernatural, over flowing love for your husband that will never die. Pray this constantly, and do not let go until God gives you just that.

—Thoughts taken from *A Rough Talk to a Stubborn Spouse* by Stephen Schwambach.

chapter
nineteen

Conclusion

To accept a situation that was so wrong has been a painful, heart-molding experience for me, but I can now thank God for His mighty hand working in the midst of each struggle. I can speak from experience when I say that Jesus brings peace.

> There is a peace that cometh after sorrow,
> Of hope surrendered, not of hope fulfilled;
> A peace that looketh not upon tomorrow,
> But calmly on a tempest that is stilled.
>
> A peace that lives not now in joy's excesses,
> Nor in the happy life of love secure;
> But in the unerring strength the heart possesses,
> Of conflicts won while learning to endure.
>
> A peace there is in sacrifices secluded,
> A life subdued, from will and passion free;
> 'Tis not the peace that over Eden brooded,
> But that which triumphed in Gethsemane.
>
> —Author unknown

I still do not have all the answers, but I have learned many lessons. Now I have a greater trust in my heavenly Father. His constant care and love outweigh all the questions I ever had. I have learned to commit all to Him. I know whatever comes He will walk through it with me. I have lived with Him long enough to know that where He leads I will follow, even if it means experiencing rejection, because I know Jesus can use it to make my life more like His.

Tests and Trials

I was rejected, cast out,
No place to call my home.
Feeling only to shout,
"Why, as I love you so dearly,
Have You allowed
In our lives
So great a cloud?"
The pain, the hurt, the struggle
Seemed far too heavy to bear.
Yet in your kindness and mercy,
You reached down to show you care."

"My child, I will be with you.
Just cast your burden all
Upon me to carry,
Lest you faint and fall."

My Lord said my tests and trials are only designed
To help me grow into His likeness and image.
And I my love to You will show.

—Matilda Kauffman

How I wish I would have known and practiced better the things I explain here while my husband and I were still together and happily married.

I conclude with a prayer of commitment by Verna Birkey from the book *Enriched Living*. This declaration brought healing to my troubled soul.

Commitment

God is my heavenly Father; He is the all-wise one Who controls all things. His essence is love, and His deepest desire is for my good. Since He is loving enough to desire only good for me, wise enough to plan just what is best, and powerful enough to accomplish what His love and goodness have planned, how can I lack any good thing? It is to You now that I surrender unconditionally all that I have and all that I am. I belong to You.

Therefore I commit myself afresh and all the demands of this day, knowing You have all the details in Your control. I purpose in my heart to thank You for whatever You allow to come to me.

Especially do I declare afresh that my husband belongs to You and not me. I have yielded to You, all rights to my husband, all rights to his time, his understanding, his attention and his love. I will take what You give back as privileges to be used for my enjoyment, and Your glory, as long as You see fit to give me these privileges.

I purposed to refuse any thoughts of self-pity, criticism, jealousy, or resentment that creep in when these precious privileges are denied—when his time is taken up by others, when he seems harsh and demanding, when he seems to have failed in consideration and love.

Lord, once again I make this declaration before You. I need You to help me be true to this commitment and to make me immediately aware of the slightest distraction. Lord, help Yourself to my life and help Yourself to my husband's life, to spend it however You chose to let him spend it, regardless of the disadvantages to me personally. Thank You for being trustworthy. In Jesus name, amen.

God knew I needed her.

Stronger THAN PAIN

Read the story of Matilda Kauffman's daughter!

This is the story of one woman's triumph over indescribable pain, multiple surgeries and multiple setbacks. Her hospital experiences were in a number of the leading universities of the eastern United States. Arlene's illness was regarded by the medical profession as extremely rare. Highly respected doctors were frustrated in their inability to find answers to this highly unusual case. In the end there were few satisfactory answers.

"Through the years of physical pain and disability, I have prayed many times that God would use me in His service and that He would create in me a heart like Jesus'. But when another cloud of pain strikes, leaving me alone and in darkness, or when I sit looking at the signature line on yet another consent form I find myself asking, 'God, where are You?'" Arlene Kauffman uttered these words that were put into the forward of her book.

Arlene Kauffman knew pain like most of us can only imagine. Her resolute faith and trust in God to the end is both remarkable and exemplary. This is a wonderful faith building book that is difficult to lay aside.

Arlene's great disappointment was to not be able to tell her father good by. She did not know where her wayward father was. This is the story of Matilda Kaufman's daughter who passed away in 2008.

KAUFFMAN | 167 PAGES | PAPERBACK | $8.99

ITEM #STR76174 | ISBN9781932676174

To order, use order form in back of the book.

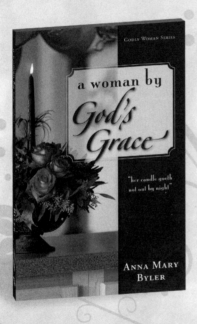

VERA'S JOURNEY

Vera's Journey was almost four years in making and begins in the year 1899. Vera was raised in a divided home. Her mother was Old Order Mennonite. Her father was Dunkard Brethren. At that time the Brethren were very strong on immersion, holding that it was necessary for salvation. These issues caused that Vera said "It was one of the most difficult periods of my life."

Vera was born in 1906, the eldest of five children. She heard the stories of the Great Titanic sinking in 1912. She knew the song of the Titanic. Vera came through two world wars. She suffered with the flu in the great epidemic of 1918 and 1919 when many lost their lives including relatives. In 1933 a son got into his father's medicine and died on the way to the hospital. He was about 17 months old. In 1944 at age 38 she got the mumps. In two or three days she was deaf, stone deaf, never to hear again. After that the family would sometimes find her in the bathroom crying. At other times they would find the towels wet with Mother's tears. Father rallied in support of Mother. When things got too difficult for her, he would say, "Mother let's go for a drive." With her loss of hearing came a constant roaring that she described as sounding like a waterfalls. This noise was with her for the last 64 years of her life. She would never hear her two youngest children cry, laugh, or sing. Vera would often say, "We need to accept what we cannot change."

"At 707 pages, 'Vera's Journey' is extensive but reads like a storybook, rich in description and history, with photos along the way. The book also has an area map, recipe cards, and Ralph and Vera's family trees. 'Vera's Journey' takes a historical look at the matriarch of a Mennonite family living in the [Shenandoah] Valley [of Virginia]."

YODER | 708 PAGES
LAMINATED HARDCOVER
$24.95

ITEM #VER76228
ISBN9781932676143

To order, use order form in back of the book.

Order Form

To order, send this completed order form to:

Vision Publishers
P.O. Box 190
Harrisonburg, VA 22803
Fax: 540-437-1969
E-mail: orders@vision-publishers.com
www.vision-publishers.com

_____ _____
Name   Date

_____ _____
Mailing Address   Phone

_____ _____
City   State   Zip

Shattered Dreams Qty. _____ x $7.99 ea. = _____

Stronger Than pain Qty. _____ x $8.99 ea. = _____

A Woman by God's Grace Qty. _____ x $8.99 ea. = _____

Vera's Journey Qty. _____ x $24.95 ea. = _____

(Please call for quantity discounts - 877-488-0901)

Price _____

Virginia residents add 5% sales tax _____

Ohio residents add applicable sales tax _____

Shipping & handling ___**$4.20**___

❑ Check #_____

❑ Money Order   ❑ Visa

Grand Total _____

❑ MasterCard   ❑ Discover   **All Payments in US Dollars**

Name on Card _____

Card # _|_|_|_|_| _|_|_|_|_| _|_|_|_|_| _|_|_|_|_|

3-digit code from signature panel _|_|_|_| Exp. Date _|_|_|_|_|

Thank you for your order!

For a complete listing of our books write for our catalog.

Bookstore inquiries welcome

Order Form

To order, send this completed order form to:

Vision Publishers
P.O. Box 190
Harrisonburg, VA 22803
Fax: 540-437-1969
E-mail: orders@vision-publishers.com
www.vision-publishers.com

_____   _____
Name   Date

_____   _____
Mailing Address   Phone

_____
City   State   Zip

Shattered Dreams Qty. _____ x $7.99 ea. = _____

Stronger Than pain Qty. _____ x $8.99 ea. = _____

A Woman by God's Grace Qty. _____ x $8.99 ea. = _____

Vera's Journey Qty. _____ x $24.95 ea. = _____

(Please call for quantity discounts - 877-488-0901)

Price _____

Virginia residents add 5% sales tax _____

Ohio residents add applicable sales tax _____

Shipping & handling __**$4.20**__

❑ Check #_____

Grand Total _____

❑ Money Order   ❑ Visa

❑ MasterCard   ❑ Discover   **All Payments in US Dollars**

Name on Card _____

Card # __|__|__|__| __|__|__|__| __|__|__|__| __|__|__|__|

3-digit code from signature panel __|__|__| Exp. Date __|__|__|__|

Thank you for your order!

For a complete listing of our books write for our catalog.

Bookstore inquiries welcome